EXPLORING COUNTRIES

Somalia

by Lisa Owings

BELLWETHER MEDIA · MINNEAPOLIS, MN

Note to Librarians, Teachers, and Parents:

Blastoff! Readers are carefully developed by literacy experts and combine standards-based content with developmentally appropriate text.

Level 1 provides the most support through repetition of high-frequency words, light text, predictable sentence patterns, and strong visual support.

Level 2 offers early readers a bit more challenge through varied simple sentences, increased text load, and less repetition of high-frequency words.

Level 3 advances early-fluent readers toward fluency through increased text and concept load, less reliance on visuals, longer sentences, and more literary language.

Level 4 builds reading stamina by providing more text per page, increased use of punctuation, greater variation in sentence patterns, and increasingly challenging vocabulary.

Level 5 encourages children to move from "learning to read" to "reading to learn" by providing even more text, varied writing styles, and less familiar topics.

Whichever book is right for your reader, Blastoff! Readers are the perfect books to build confidence and encourage a love of reading that will last a lifetime!

This edition first published in 2015 by Bellwether Media, Inc.

Library of Congress Cataloging-in-Publication Data

Owings, Lisa.
  Somalia / by Lisa Owings.
     pages cm. – (Blastoff! readers. Exploring countries)
  Includes bibliographical references and index.
  Summary: "Developed by literacy experts for students in grades three through seven, this book introduces young readers to the geography and culture of Somalia"– Provided by publisher.
  Audience: Ages 7-12.
  ISBN 978-1-62617-177-0 (hardcover : alk. paper)
  1. Somalia–Juvenile literature. I. Title. II. Series: Blastoff! Readers. 5, Exploring Countries.
  DT401.5.O85 2015
  967.73–dc23
                                                              2014034774

Printed in the United States of America, North Mankato, MN.

Contents

Somalia is the easternmost country on Africa's **mainland**. Shaped like the number 7, it covers 246,201 square miles (637,657 square kilometers) on the **Horn of Africa**. Somalia shares most of its western border with Ethiopia. Kenya lies to the southwest. A small part of the country's northwestern border touches Djibouti.

Somalia has the second-longest coastline in Africa. Its northern shores dip into the **Gulf** of Aden, which separates the country from the Arabian **Peninsula**. The Indian Ocean stretches along Somalia's eastern coast. Mogadishu is Somalia's capital city. It stands along the Indian Ocean in the southeastern part of the country.

N
W **E**
S

Djibouti

Gulf of Aden

Somalia

Ethiopia

Indian
Ocean

Kenya

Mogadishu
⭐

Did you know?

Somaliland and Puntland are
self-governing regions in northern
Somalia. They were formed in the 1990s
after the fall of Somalia's government.

Did you know?
Somalia has two dry seasons and two rainy seasons each year.

Somalia is a land of flat, grassy **plains** and **arid** weather. It is hottest and driest along the northern coast. Shrubs dot this sandy, desert-like area called the Guban. Rivers appear only when it rains. South of the Guban, mountains stretch from east to west. Their peaks include Mount Shimbiris, Somalia's highest at 7,900 feet (2,400 meters).

Jubba River

Grassy **plateaus** cover most of the center of the country. **Nomadic** Somalis travel over them, following their herds of **grazing** livestock. The land becomes greener to the south. Much-needed water for farmland flows from the Jubba and Shabeelle Rivers. Land near the Kenyan border is thickly shaded by thorny bushes and acacia trees.

The Laas Geel caves in Somaliland are full of beauty and history. The surrounding area is flat and dry, with scattered trees and bushes clinging to life. Camels and tortoises move slowly across the landscape. A granite **outcrop** rises between two dried-up riverbeds. This rocky hill hides one of the greatest treasures in Africa.

Near the top of the outcrop are several caves with smooth, colorful walls. A closer look reveals that the walls are covered in paintings. They show peaceful scenes of people living among cattle and other animals. The paintings are thought to be between 5,000 and 11,000 years old. Somalia's dry climate has kept their colors vibrant through the centuries.

fun fact
Laas Geel means "camel watering hole" in Somali.

giraffes

Many animals roam over Somalia's plains. Large mammals are found in southern Somalia. Lions, leopards, and cheetahs stalk prey through tall grasses. Hyenas prowl the grasslands at night. Herds of antelopes and ostriches have to be quick to avoid these predators. A small number of giraffes pluck leaves from acacia trees.

hyena

ostrich

frankincense

fun fact

Frankincense and myrrh trees thrive in Somalia. The fragrant sap of these trees has been used in perfume since ancient times.

Birds fill Somalian skies. Larks can be heard singing, and bustards run along the ground. Water birds such as herons and gulls are also common. Chameleons hide in the trees. On the ground, tortoises show off their patterned shells. Nile crocodiles live in the country's rivers. On **coral reefs** off the coast, peaceful dugongs and sea turtles swim alongside fierce sharks.

11

Over 10 million people call Somalia home. More than eight out of every ten are **native** to the area. They speak the Somali language and practice the religion of Islam. Other people living in Somalia include the Bantu, another African group with their own language. Some 30,000 Arabs and a small number of Italians also live in the country.

Although most Somalis share the same culture, they are divided into **clans**. These family groups come from the same **ancestors**. For decades, Somali clans have fought one another in a **civil war**. The war has deeply affected life in Somalia. A new government in power since 2012 brings hope for peace.

Speak Somali!

English	Somali	How to say it
hello	iska warran	is-KAH WAHR-ahn
good-bye	nabad gelyo	nah-bahd GEHL-yoh
yes	haa	HA-ah
no	maya	MAY-ah
please	fadlan	FUDD-llan
thank you	mahad sanid	mah-HAHD SAH-need
friend	saaxiib	sah-HEEB

Did you know?
Nomadic Somali boys usually begin herding camels around age 13.

More than half of Somalis live in the countryside. Most are nomads who move with their herds of camels, goats, sheep, or cattle. Nomadic Somalis live in dome-shaped huts called *aqal*. These homes are easy to take apart and transport. Other Somalis live on farms. They build round homes out of mud.

Large numbers of Somalis are settling in cities each year. **Urban** families live in modern homes made of stone or cinder blocks. Most Somalis shop and trade at open-air markets. Mogadishu offers stores and shopping centers. To get from place to place, people usually walk or rely on animals. Vans and trucks carry people and goods over paved roads.

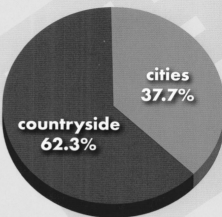

Where People Live in Somalia

cities 37.7%

countryside 62.3%

War has made it hard for Somali children to go to school. The countryside has few schools. Children in northern Somalia and major cities have a better chance at an education. Fewer than half of Somali children begin school, and even fewer continue beyond elementary school. Many parents cannot afford lessons or losing extra help at home. However, people around the world are working to help more Somali children attend school.

Somalis who do attend school learn to read, write, and do math. Some study the Quran, the holy book of Islam. A few continue on to high school. They may then attend college, often in Mogadishu. Other students choose schools that teach them how to do specific jobs.

Where People Work
in Somalia

manufacturing/
services 29%

farming 71%

Farming is the most common job in Somalia. About seven out of every ten Somalis raise crops or livestock. Most tend herds of camels, goats, sheep, or cattle. They sell some of the meat and skins to other countries. Crop farmers usually grow just enough food to feed their families. However, some work on large **plantations**. They grow bananas, sugarcane, or sorghum. Somali fishers catch tuna and mackerel for canning.

Few factories remain in Somali cities. However, some Somalis still work to process sugar, make clothing, or provide phone services. Many others make crafts to sell at markets. Wood carvings, leather work, and woven cloth are both beautiful and useful.

Somalis enjoy spending free time with friends and family. Women enjoy visiting one another's homes, while men gather at tea shops to talk and play board games. Somalis love to tell stories, recite poems, and sing songs. Other **traditional** activities include folk dancing and putting on plays or talent shows.

Many Somalis enjoy playing or watching soccer. Children usually make their own balls out of whatever is available. Other popular children's games include basketball, volleyball, and skipping or jumping games. In the evenings, families often listen to the radio. Larger cities offer modern entertainment such as television, movie theaters, and the Internet.

Did you know?

Guests in a Somali home should not eat all the food on their plates. Leaving a few bites lets the hosts know they have offered enough food.

Somalis eat mainly grains and animal products. *Anjero* is a common breakfast food. This pancake-like bread is often topped with butter and sugar. Families gather at home for a large midday meal. They enjoy rice with goat or camel meat. Italian-style pasta with meat sauce is also popular. Bananas are often served as a side.

Fried pastries called *sambuus* are a tasty snack between meals. For dinner, cornbread patties called *muufo* are made in a clay oven. They can be served with beans, soup, or salad. A classic Somali dessert is *halwa*. It is a jelly-like sweet made with sugar, spices, and sometimes nuts. Many Somalis also drink spicy tea called *shaah* throughout the day.

sambuus

halwa

fun fact

Nomadic Somalis often have fresh camel's milk for breakfast and dinner.

Most holidays in Somalia are religious. During the holy month of Ramadan, Somalis **fast** between sunrise and sunset. At night, they feast with their loved ones. *Eid al-Fitr* is the celebration at the end of Ramadan. Children dress in new clothes, visit family and friends, and enjoy gifts and sweets. During *Eid al-Adha*, wealthy families share meat with their neighbors.

Somalis also celebrate many different New Years. They mark the beginning of the calendar year on January 1. In the spring, they celebrate the Persian New Year. The date of the Islamic New Year changes each year.

Eid al-Fitr

Did you know?

Somali rapper K'naan first wrote the song "Wavin' Flag" about his hopes for his home country. It became world-famous when it was used for the 2010 FIFA World Cup.

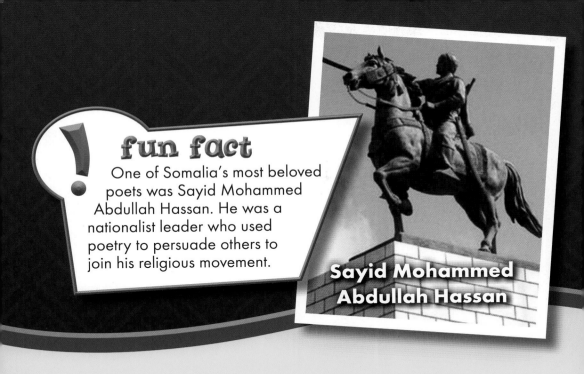

fun fact

One of Somalia's most beloved poets was Sayid Mohammed Abdullah Hassan. He was a nationalist leader who used poetry to persuade others to join his religious movement.

Sayid Mohammed Abdullah Hassan

To Somalis, poetry is far more than art. It is a major part of the national identity and how people express themselves. Somalis did not have a written alphabet until 1972. They shared and learned everything through speaking, listening, and remembering. Spoken poetry is still their most respected way of communicating.

Somalis use poetry to discuss everything important to them. Poetry can stop fights between clans or sway political decisions. It teaches lessons and congratulates newlyweds. People also use it to offer humor, comfort, or advice. The tradition of poetry suffered during the war. However, many Somalis believe that bringing back poetry can heal their country. They believe well-chosen words can bring peace.

Fast Facts About Somalia

Somalia's Flag

Somalia's flag is light blue with a white star in the center. The colors honor the United Nations flag. The five points of the star represent the five Somali homelands in northern Somalia, southern Somalia, Djibouti, Ethiopia, and Kenya. This flag was adopted in 1954.

Official Name: Federal Republic of Somalia

Area: 246,201 square miles (637,657 square kilometers); Somalia is the 44th largest country in the world.

Capital City:	Mogadishu
Important Cities:	Hargeysa, Berbera, Kismaayo
Population:	10,428,043 (July 2014)
Official Languages:	Somali, Arabic
National Holiday:	Independence Day (July 1)
Religion:	Islam (Sunni Muslim)
Major Industries:	farming, fishing
Natural Resources:	coal, iron ore, uranium, copper, salt, natural gas
Manufactured Products:	sugar, clothing, crafts
Farm Products:	cattle, sheep, goats, fish, bananas, sugarcane, sorghum, corn
Unit of Money:	Somali shilling; one shilling is divided into 100 cents.

Glossary

ancestors—relatives who lived long ago

arid—very dry

civil war—a war between different groups within the same country

clans—large groups of families who have common ancestors and are loyal to one another

coral reefs—structures made of coral that usually grow in shallow seawater

fast—to choose not to eat

grazing—feeding on grass

gulf—part of an ocean or sea that extends into land

Horn of Africa—the horn-shaped part of eastern Africa including Somalia, Ethiopia, and parts of surrounding countries

mainland—the continent or the main part of a continent

native—originally from a specific place

nomadic—having no specific home and traveling from place to place

outcrop—part of a rock formation that rises above the ground

peninsula—a section of land that extends out from a larger piece of land and is almost completely surrounded by water

plains—large areas of flat land

plantations—large farms that grow coffee beans, cotton, rubber, or other crops; plantations are mainly found in warm climates.

plateaus—areas of flat, raised land

traditional—related to a custom, idea, or belief handed down from one generation to the next

urban—relating to cities and city life

To Learn More

AT THE LIBRARY

Gelletly, LeeAnne. *Somalia*. Broomall, Penn.: Mason Crest Pub., 2010.

Hamilton, Janice. *Somalia in Pictures*. Minneapolis, Minn.: Twenty-First Century Books, 2007.

Laird, Elizabeth. *The Ogress and the Snake and Other Stories from Somalia*. London: Frances Lincoln Children's Books, 2009.

ON THE WEB

Learning more about Somalia is as easy as 1, 2, 3.

1. Go to www.factsurfer.com.

2. Enter "Somalia" into the search box.

3. Click the "Surf" button and you will see a list of related web sites.

With factsurfer.com, finding more information is just a click away.

Index

The images in this book are reproduced through the courtesy of: Shabele Media/ Corbis, front cover;
Vladislav Galenko, pp. 6-7, 15, 16-17; DeAgostini/ SuperStock, p. 7; Andrew McConnell/ Alamy,
pp. 8-9; ChrisVanLennepPhoto, pp. 10-11; Enrique Ramos, p. 11 (top); Ryan M. Bolton, p. 11 (middle);
Vladimir Melnik, p. 11 (bottom); Patrick Aventurier/ Getty Images, p. 12; Eric Lafforgue/ Alamy, p. 14;
Liba Taylor/ Glow Images, pp. 18, 19 (right); Kevin Fleming/ Corbis, p. 19 (left); AFP/ Getty Images,
pp. 20, 21; Eye Ubiquitous/ SuperStock, p. 22; Dereje, p. 23 (left); HLPhoto, p. 23 (right); Mohamed
Sheikh Nor/ AP Images, pp. 24-25; Somali Government/ Wikipedia, p. 27; Maisei Raman, p. 28;
Glyn Thomas/ Alamy, p. 29.

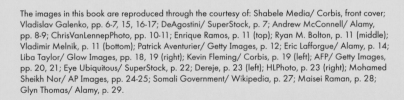